52 Sex Coupons

For Him

♥ **BELONGS TO:**
....

Good For One

Wake Your

Partner

Up With

Oral

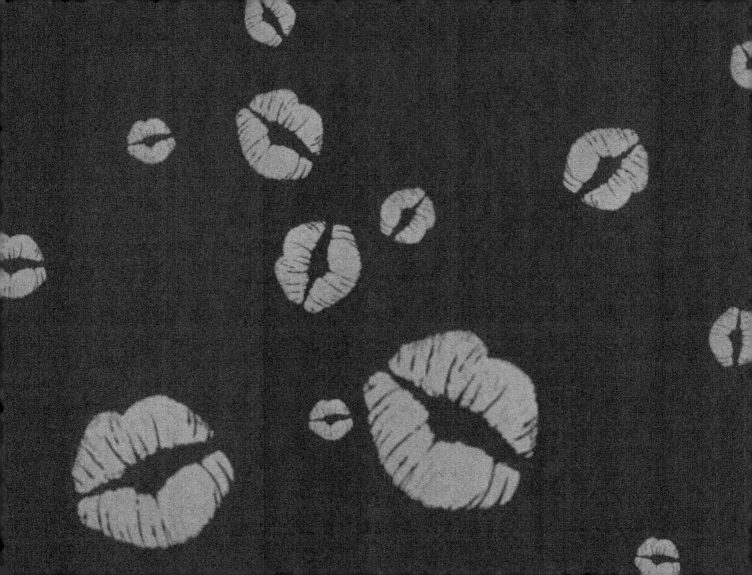

Good For One

I Really Want to Kiss You, And Not Just On The Lips

Good For One

Pick a Fantasy

ROLEPLAY

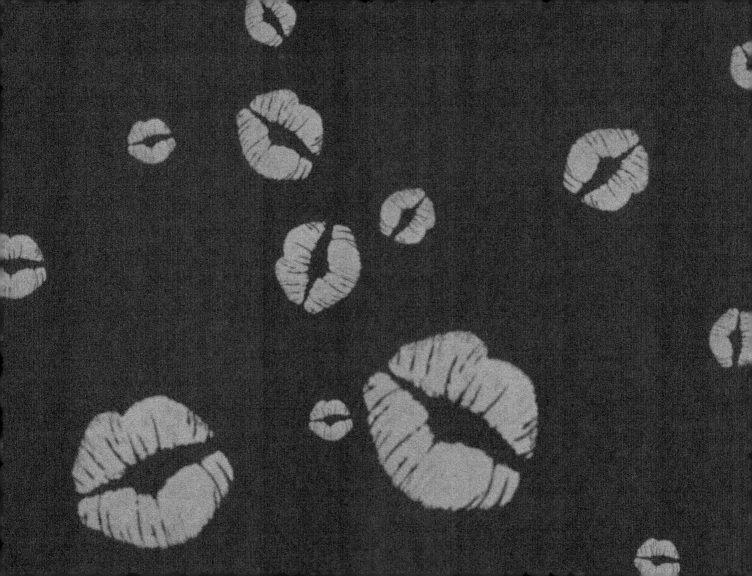

Good For One

When you're in the Mood

TO SIT BACK, RELAX

& WATCH ME

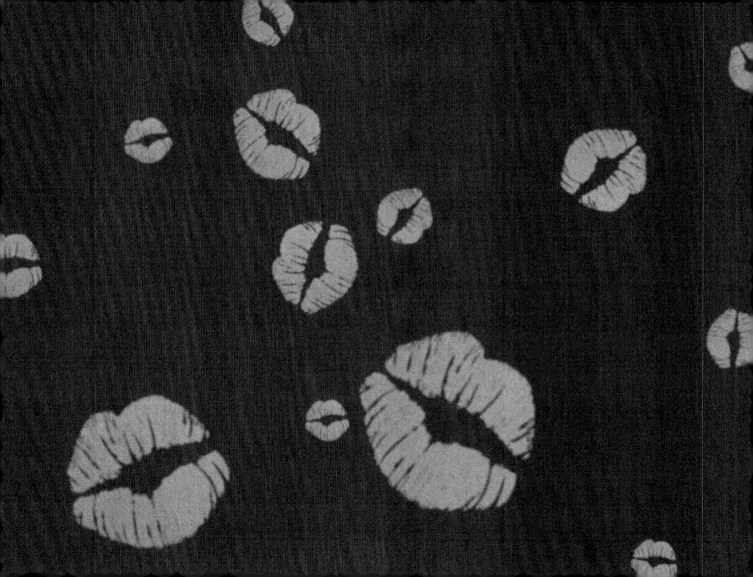

Good For One

Strip Poker

GAME

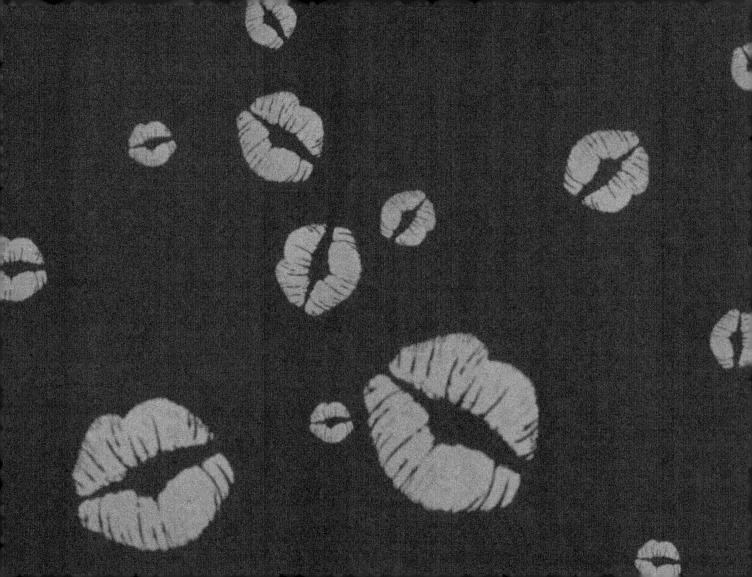

Good For One

Eat My pussy

Really Slow likes

It's the Best Meal

You've Ever Had

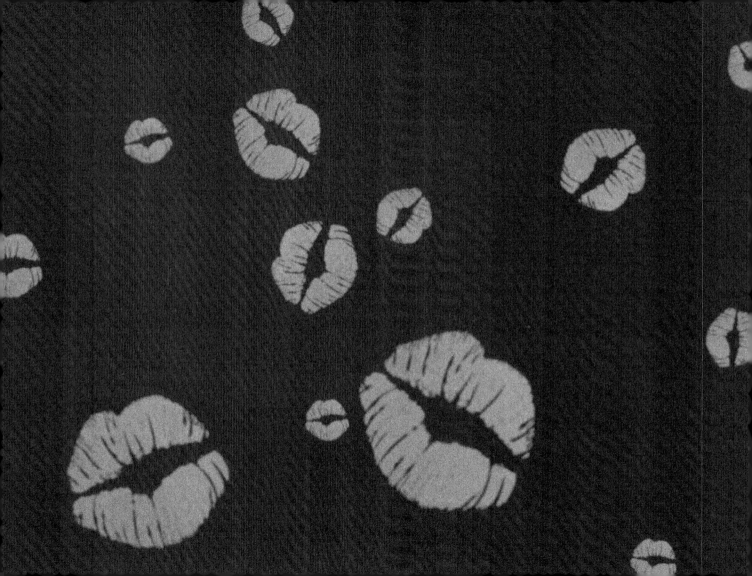

Good For One

Three Sexy

WISHES

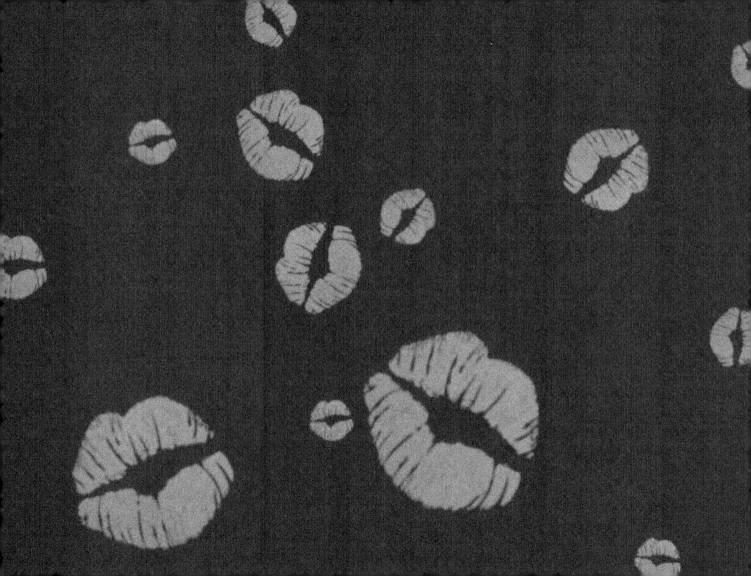

Good For One

Finding

The G-Spot

Orgasm

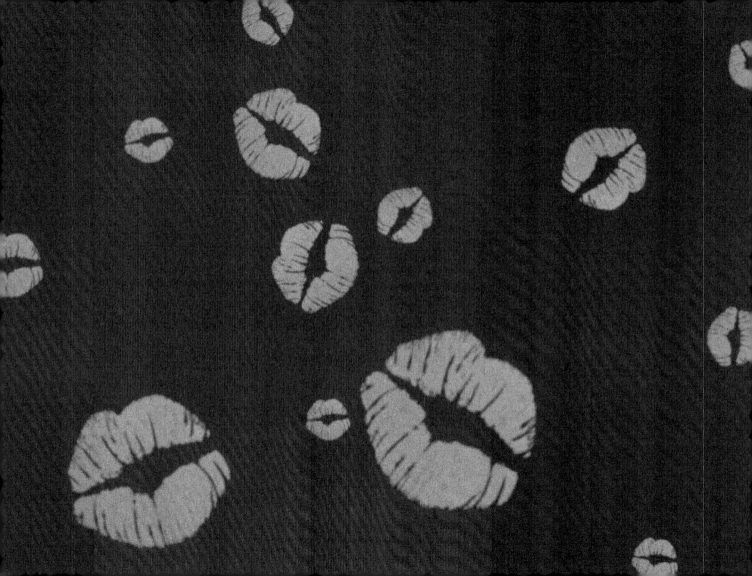

Good For One

A Hawaiian

STRIP TEASE

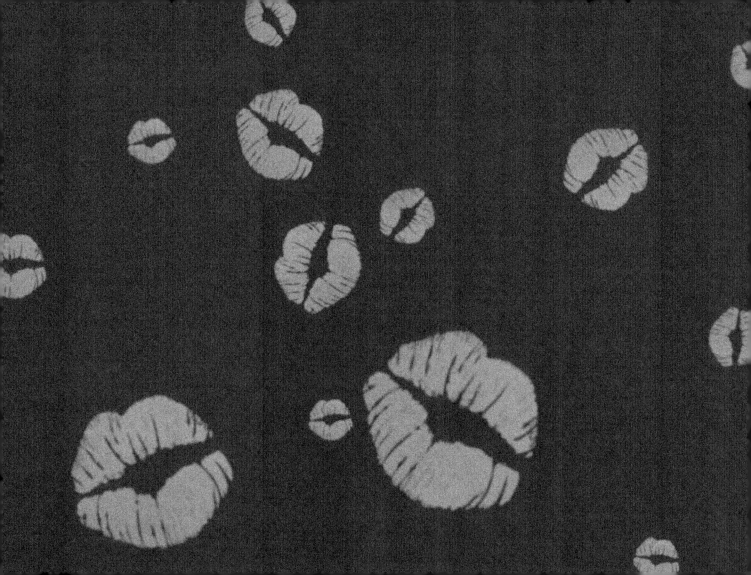

Good For One

Sensual

Massage

Good For One

Swear to Me,

You Won't Stop

UNTIL MY LEGS ARE SHAKING

&

THE NEIGHBORS KNOW

YOUR NAME. "

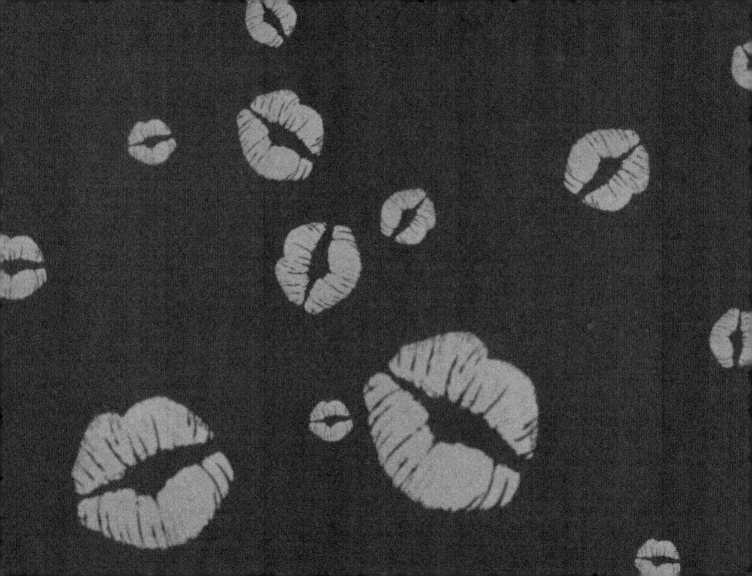

Good For One

Whip Cream

OR

Chocolate

SOME ADVENTURE

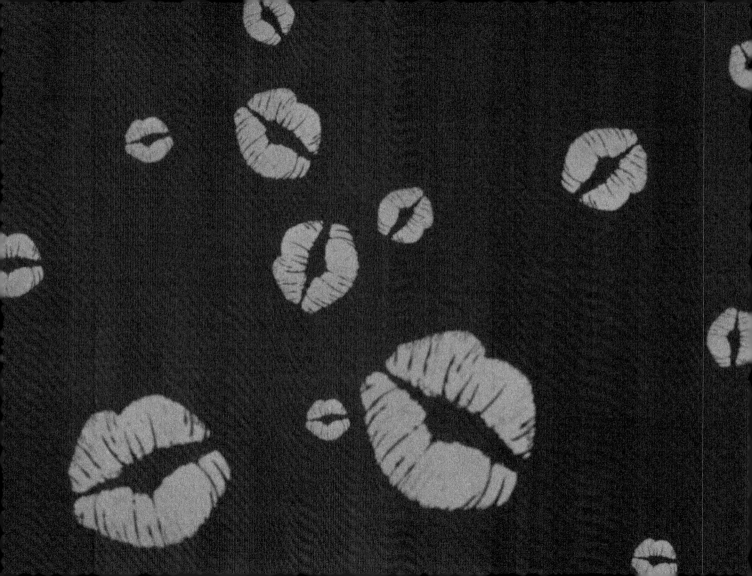

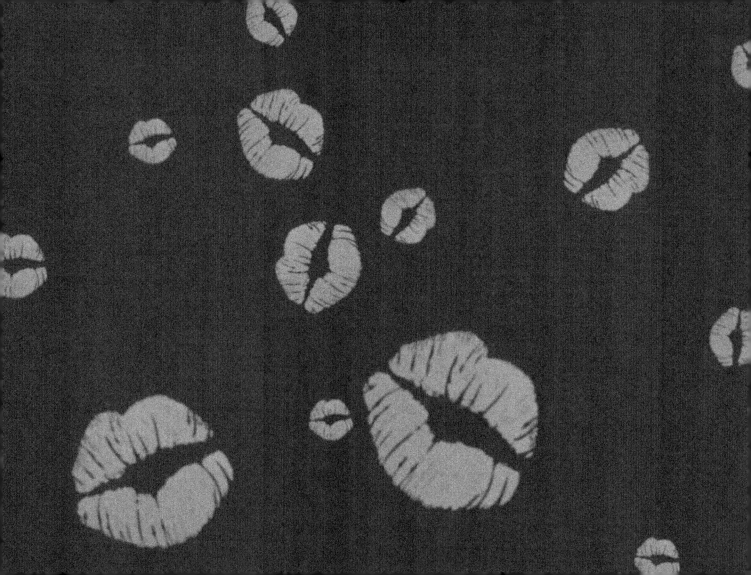

Good For One

A Skinny Dipping

ADVENTURE

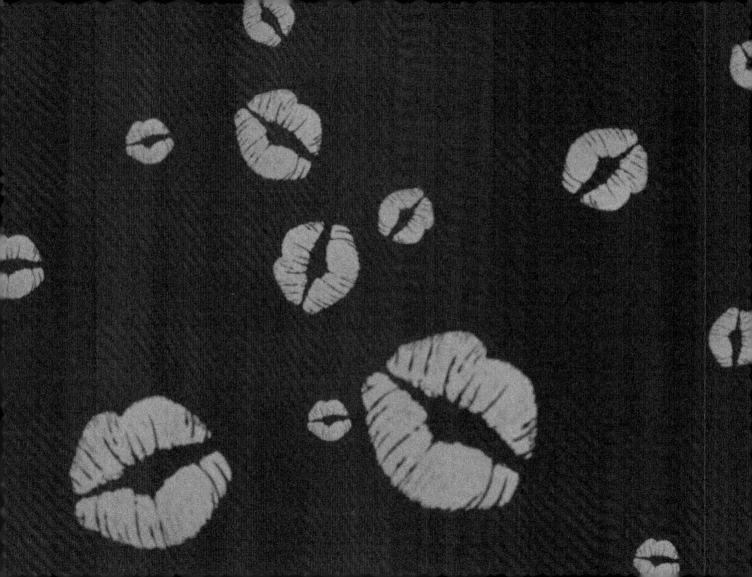

Good For One

A Role

PLAYING

SESSION

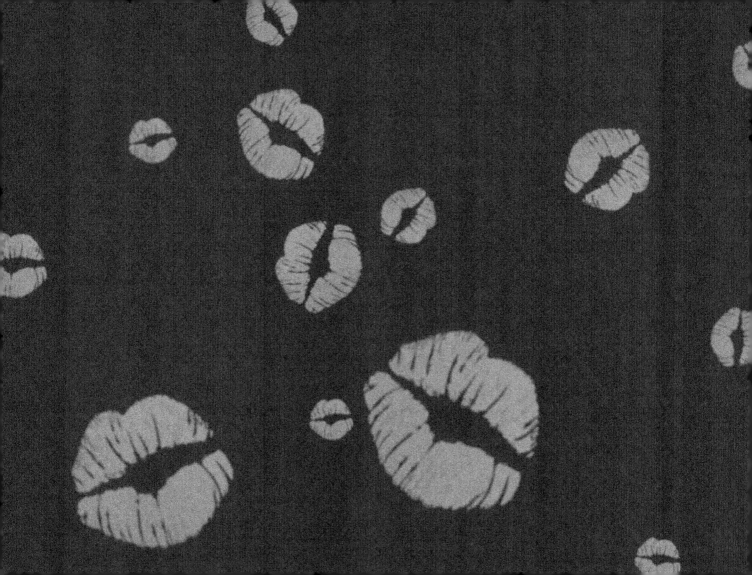

Good For One

Let's Do It Slowly

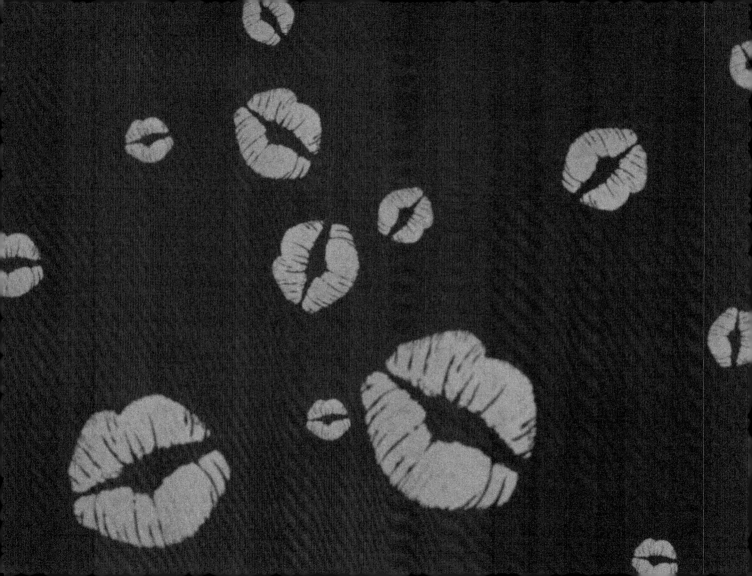

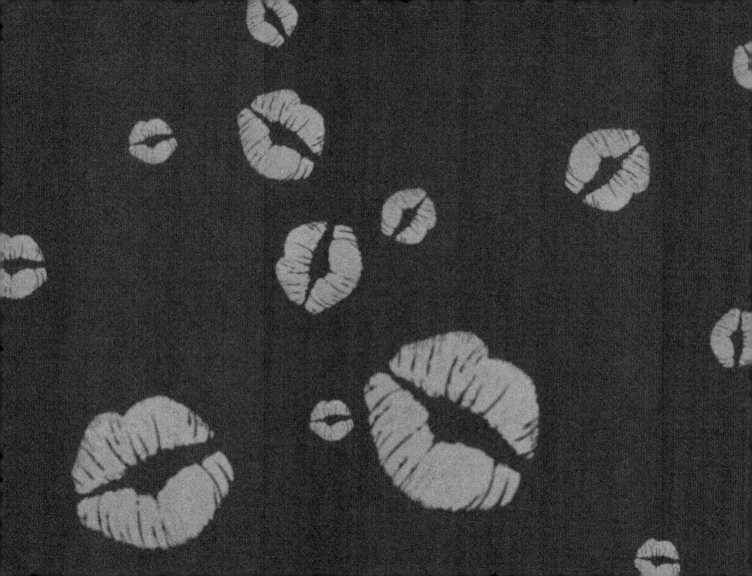

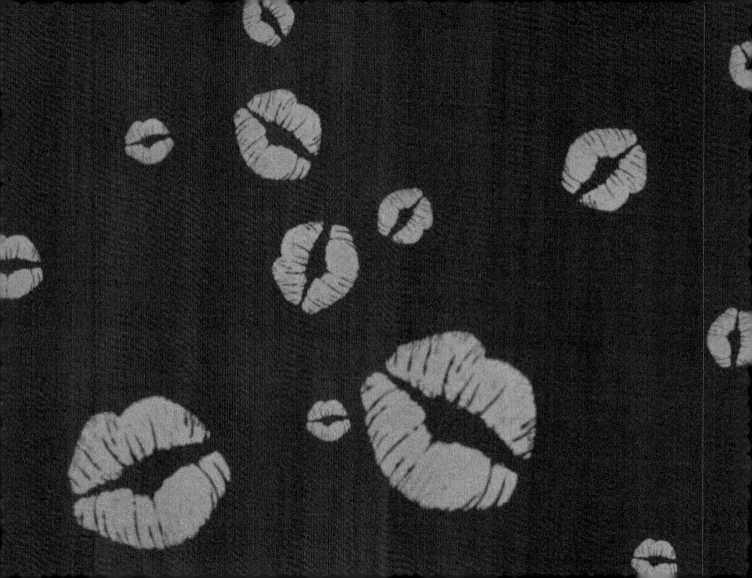

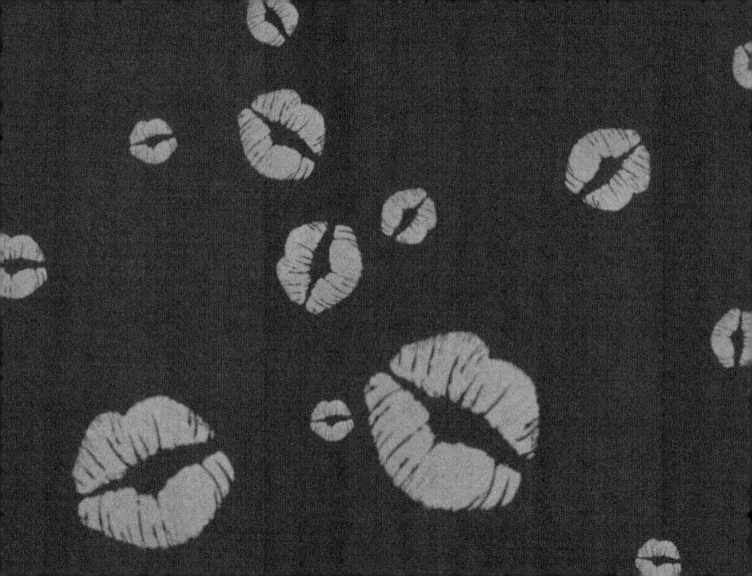

Good For One

A Dirty Dance

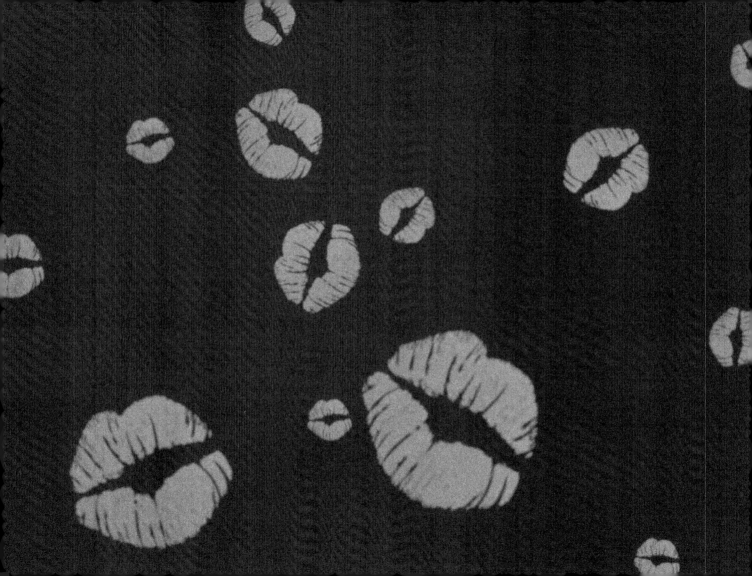

Good For One

Your pants

bother me!

Take

them off

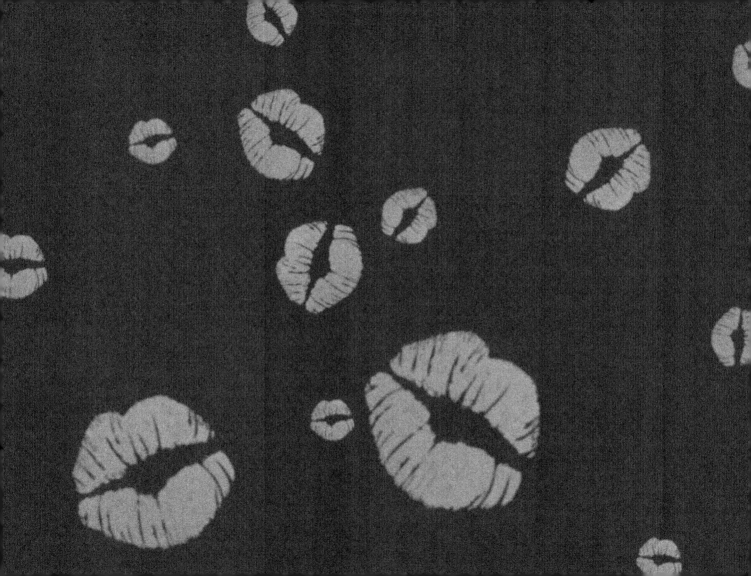

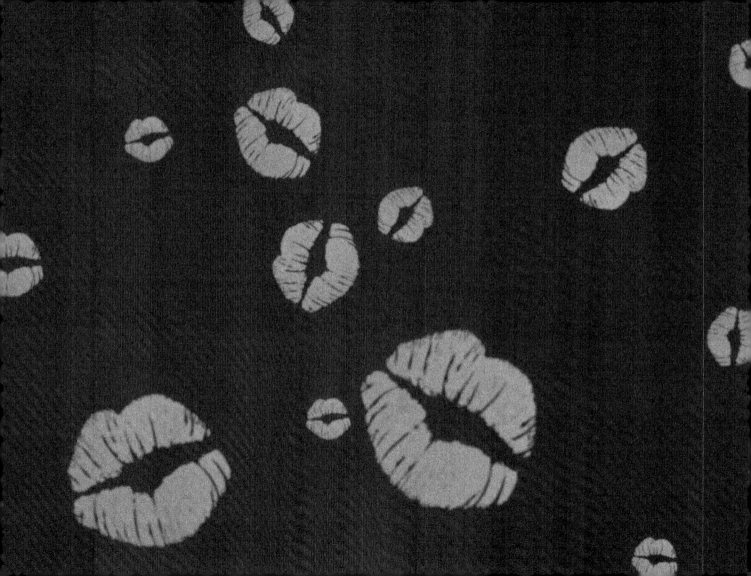

Good For One

GET THE COCONUT OIL

OUT IT'S ABOUT TO

GET REAL FILTHY LAY

ON YOUR TUMMY

WHILE

I OIL UP YOUR

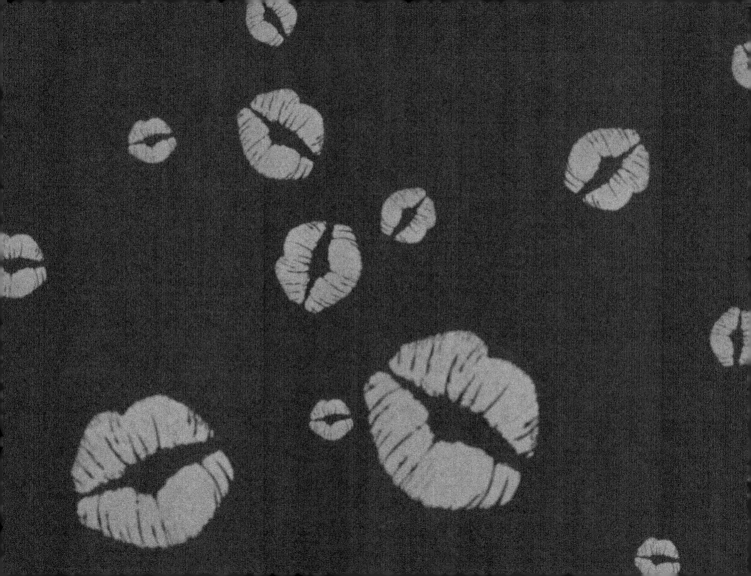

Good For One

*Give Me
the Best Blow job
You've Ever
Given!*

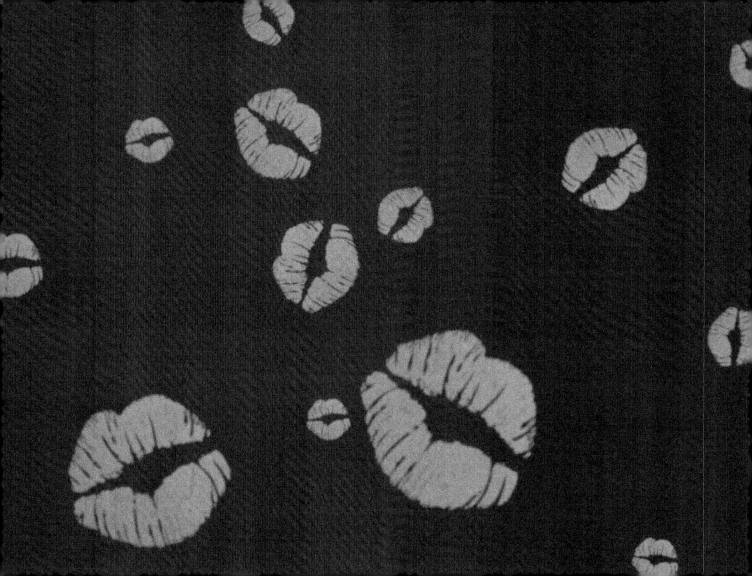

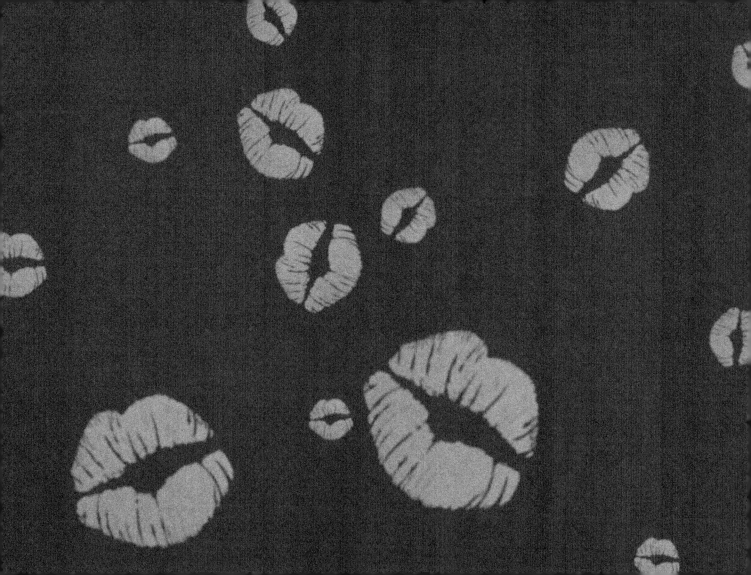

Good For One

My Sexiest Fantasy

PLAYED OUT RIGHT IN FRONT OF ME

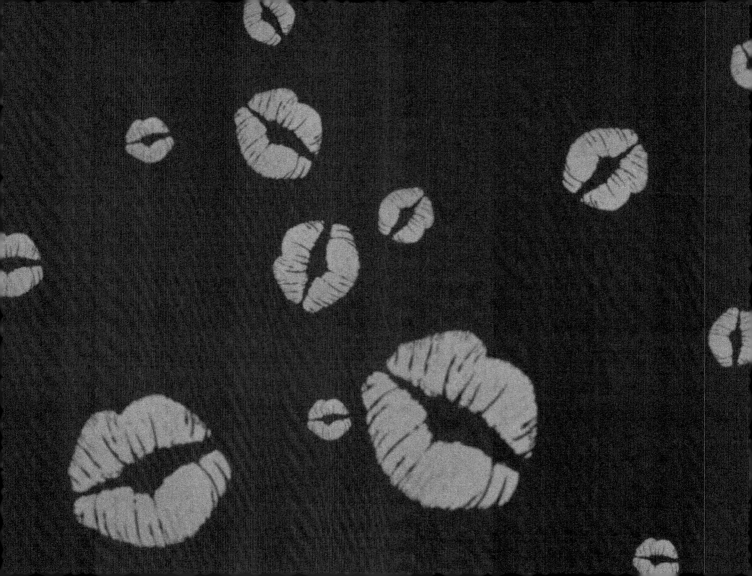

Good For One

Candlelit

Bubble

Bath

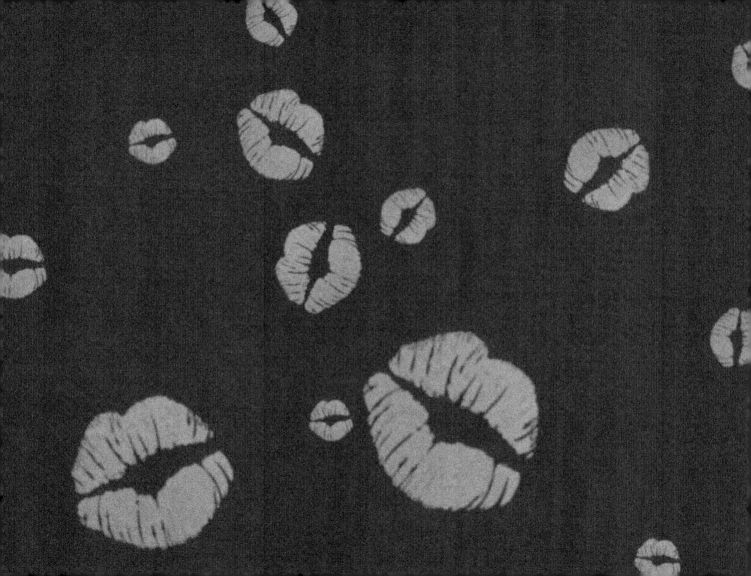

Good For One

Tender

Sweet Sex

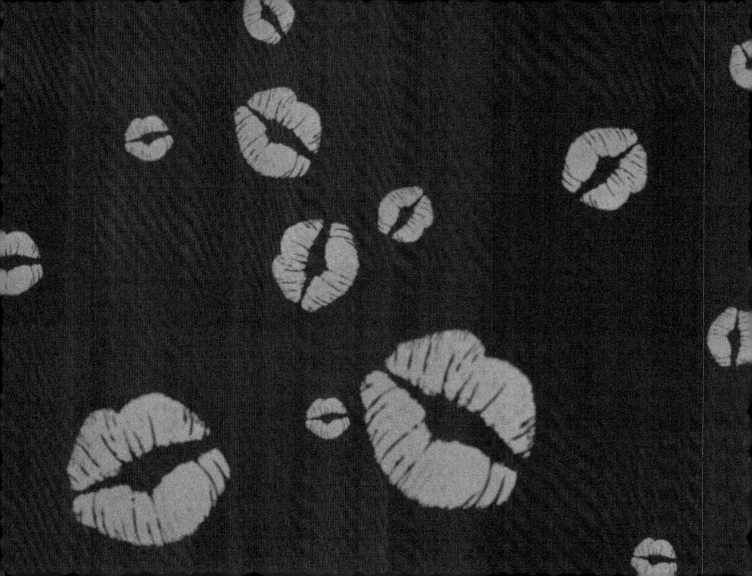

Good For One

Orgasm

Without

Sex

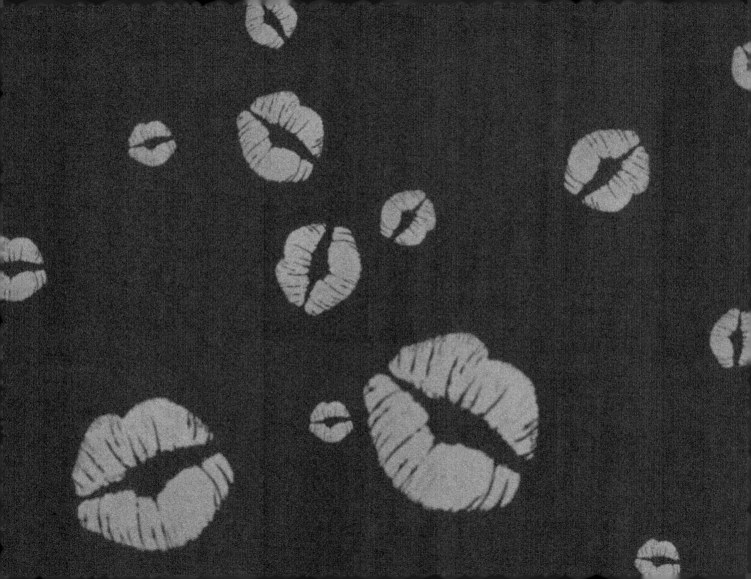

Good For One

Sensual

LAP DANCE

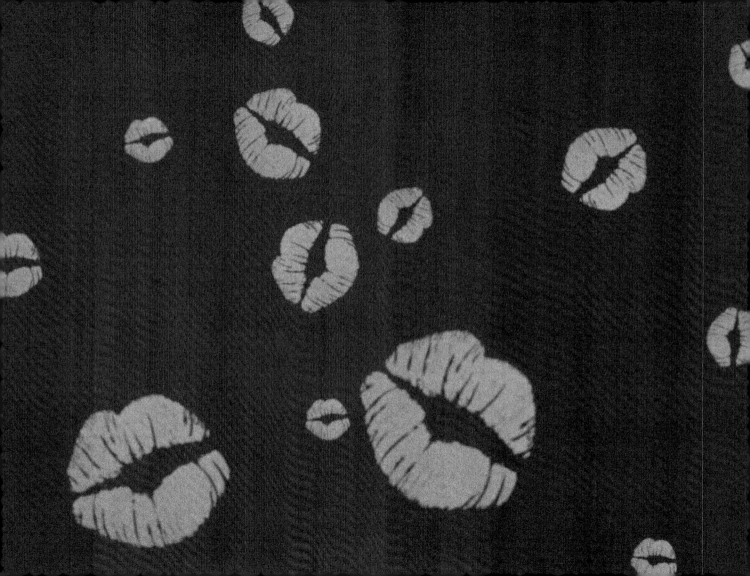

Good For One

Oral Pleasure

THE WAY YOU LIKE

IT

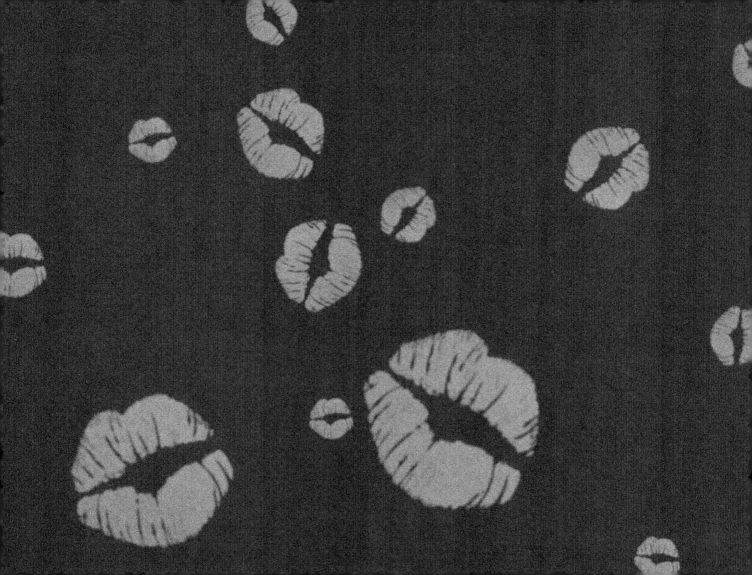

Good For One

Sex

Outdoor

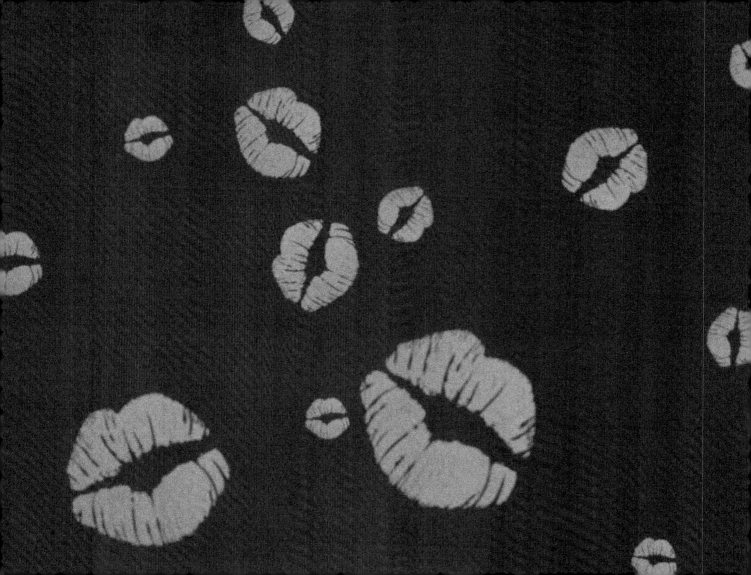

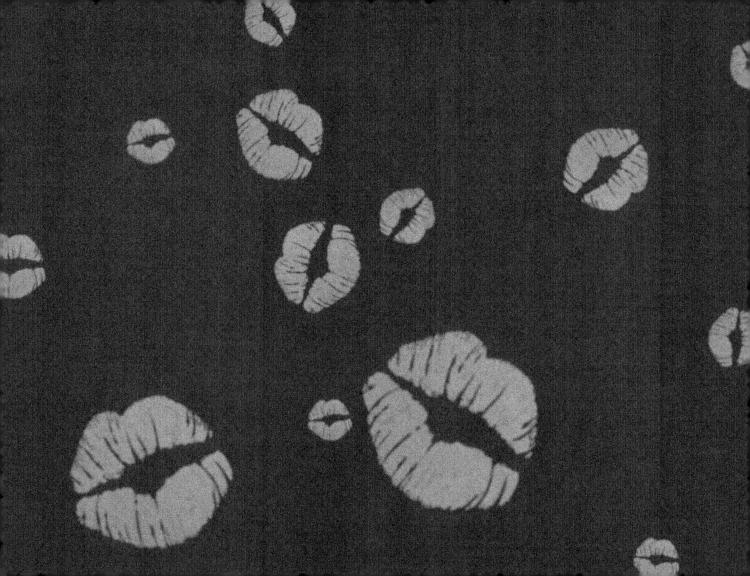

Good For One

a Night Of Rest
& Relaxation

MY MOUTH WILL DO

ALL THE WORK

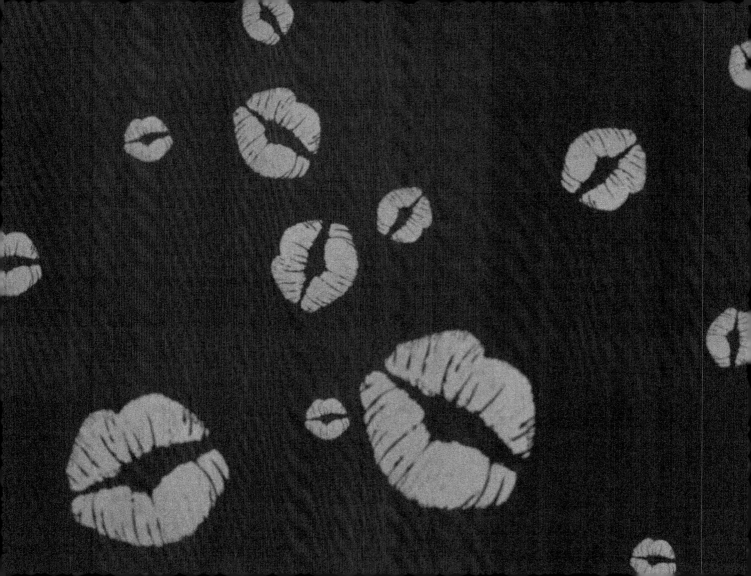

Good For One

Quickie

ANY TIME YOU WANT

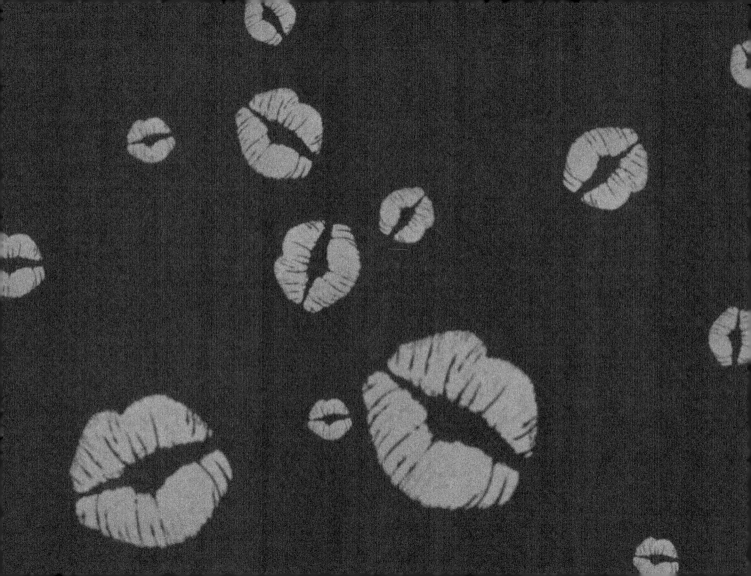

Good For One

I Want More.

More Rough Sex. More

Love. More Cuddles.

**I want more of
everything with
you**

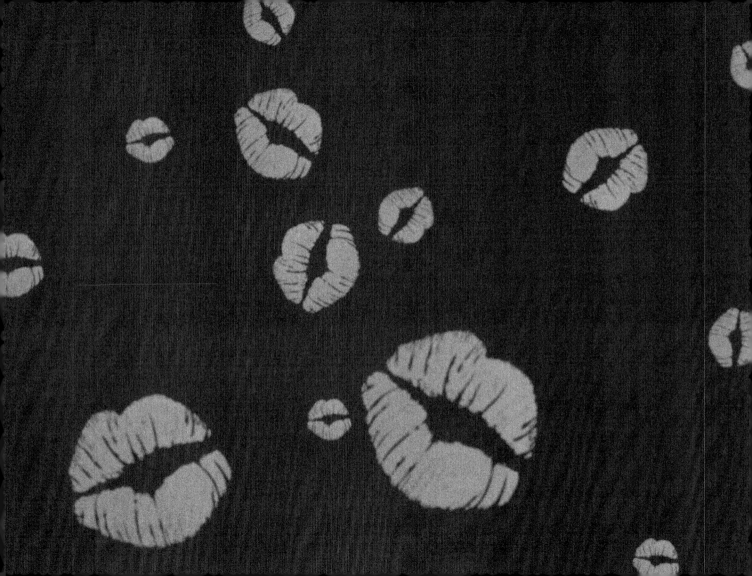

Good For One

Have

Crazy

Loud Sex

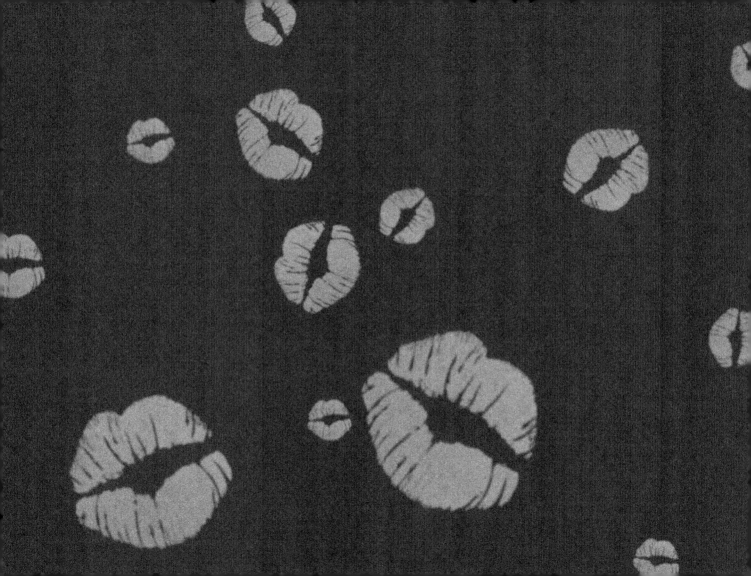

Good For One

LaZy Sex

LAZY MISSIONARY.

Lazy Penis Rubs.

LAZY CLITORIS

STIMULATION.

Just Relax

AND THEN...

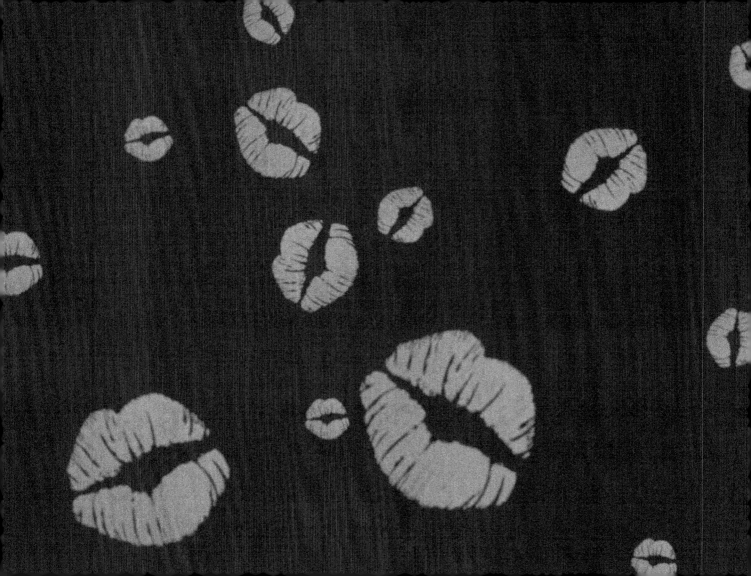

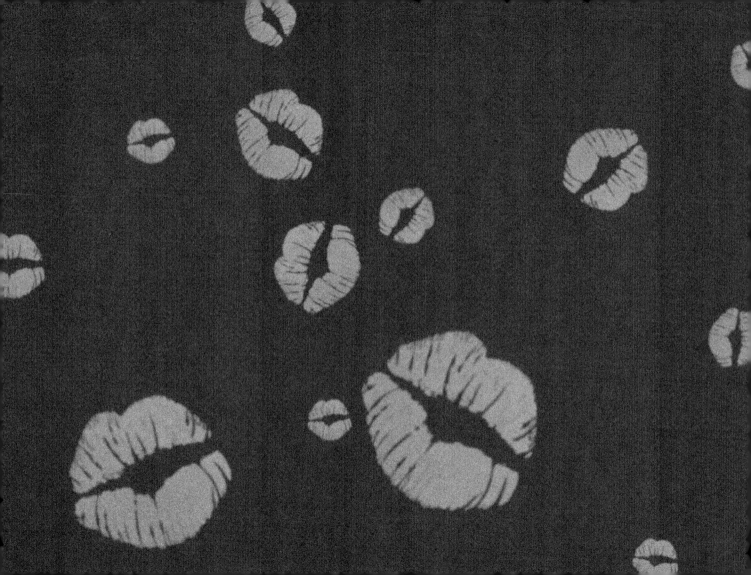

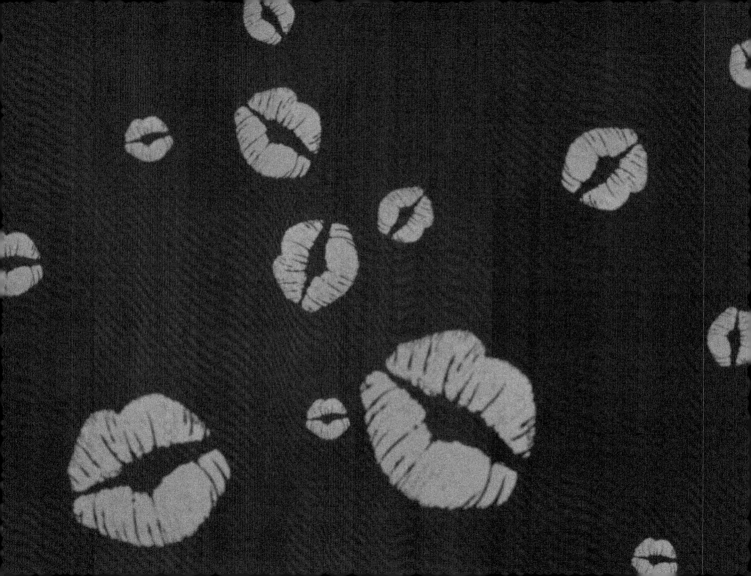

Good For One

Masturbate in front of each other

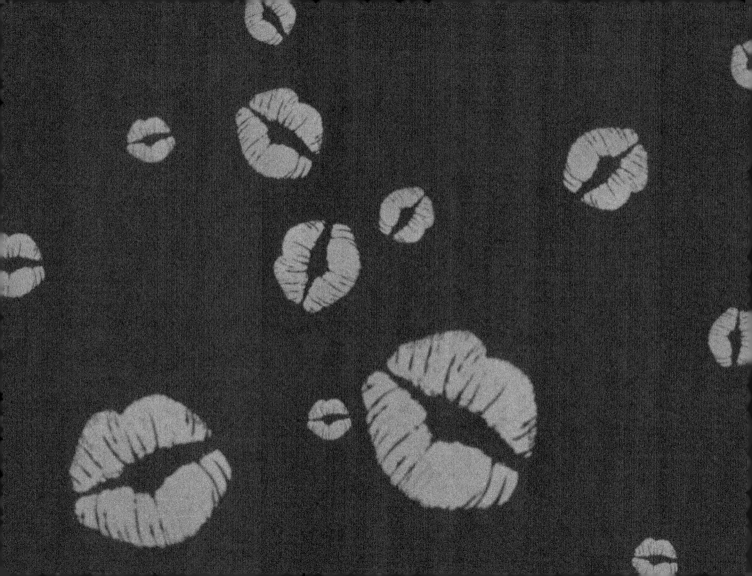

Good For One

Suck on my breasts & play

with them for

20 minutes

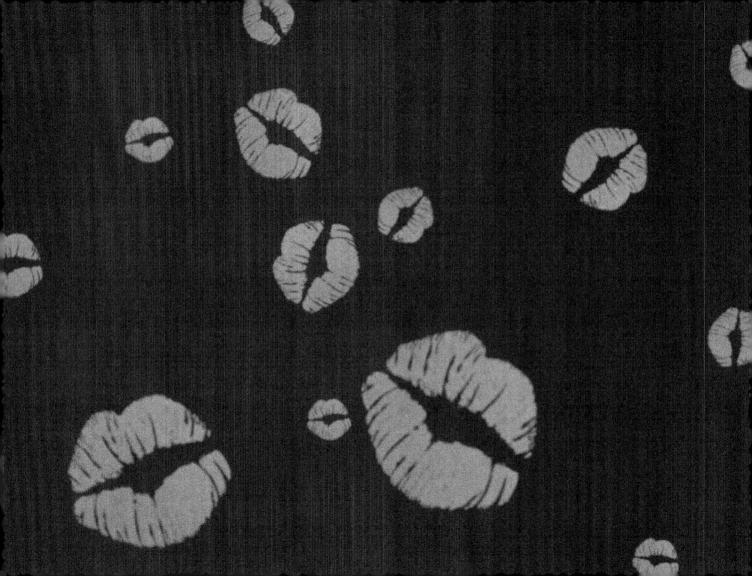

Good For One

A Sex Toy Together

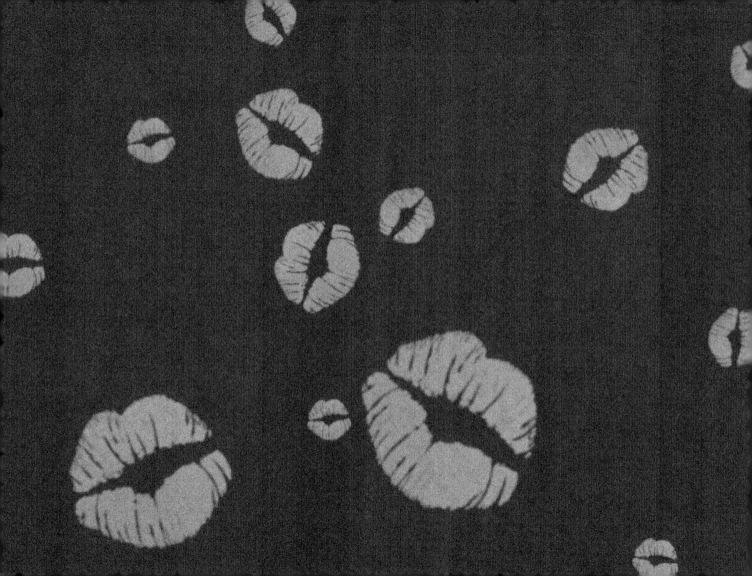

Good For One

Three Cosmo Sex Positions In One Session

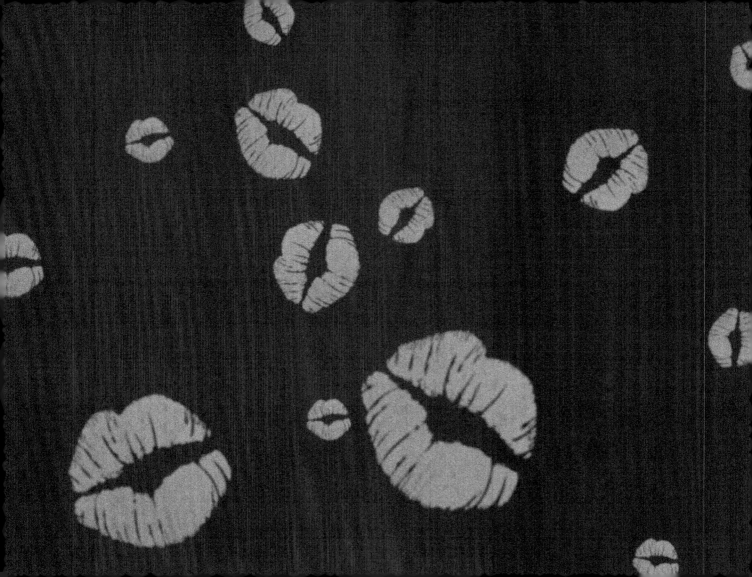

Good For One

Ice Cube Blow Jobs

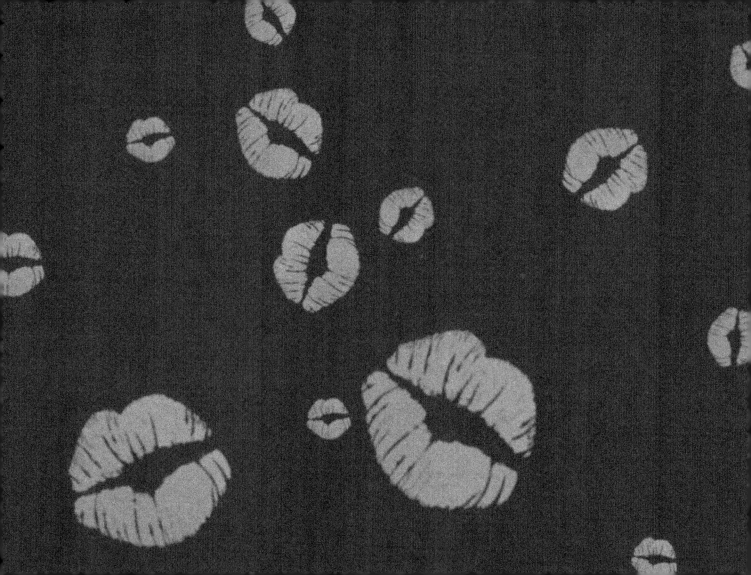

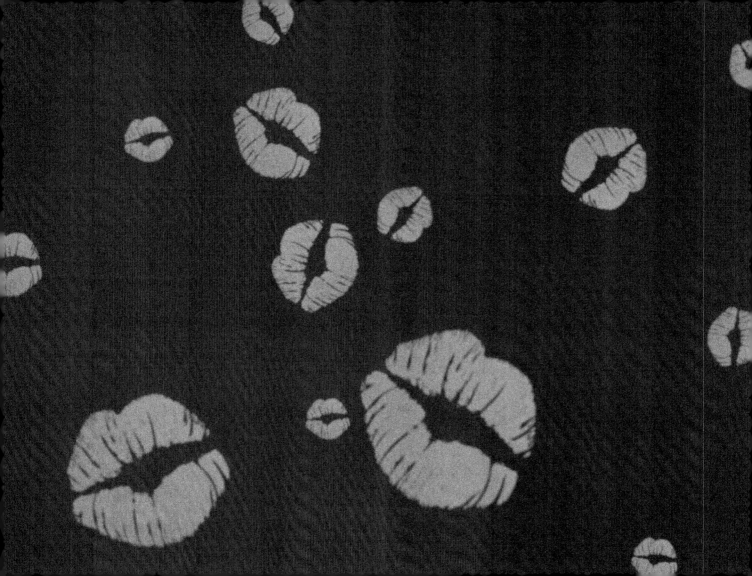

Good For One

Talking

Dirty

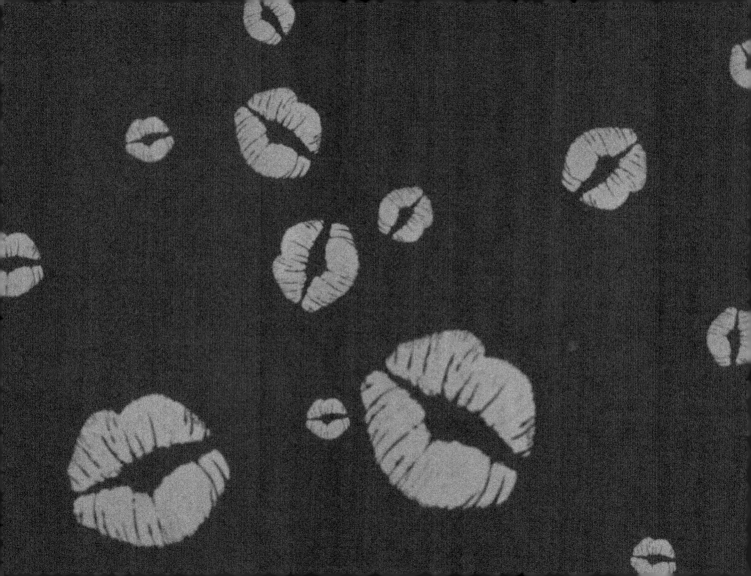

Good For One

I Want You SO

Fuking Much

I'm Gonna Go

CraZy!

Good For One

Have Sex In the Morning

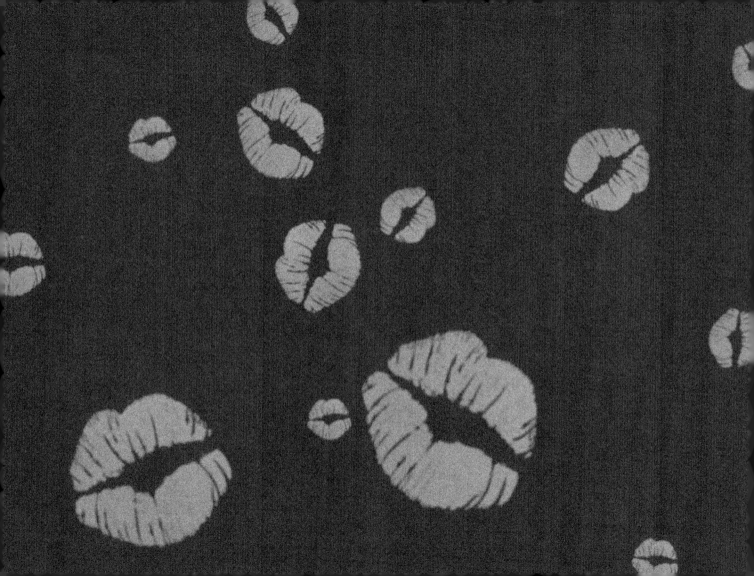

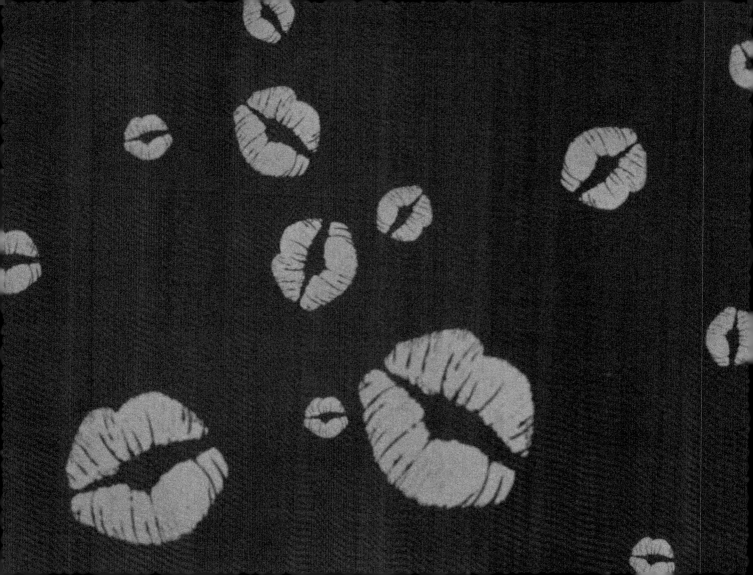

Good For One

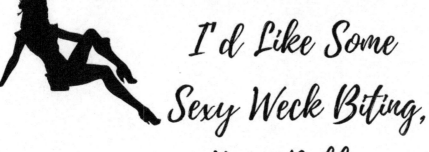

I'd Like Some

Sexy Weck Biting,

Hair-Pulling,

Butt Spanking,

Back Scratching

Sex please

Good For One

I Promise to
Always
Be By Your Side.
Or Under you.
Or On top.

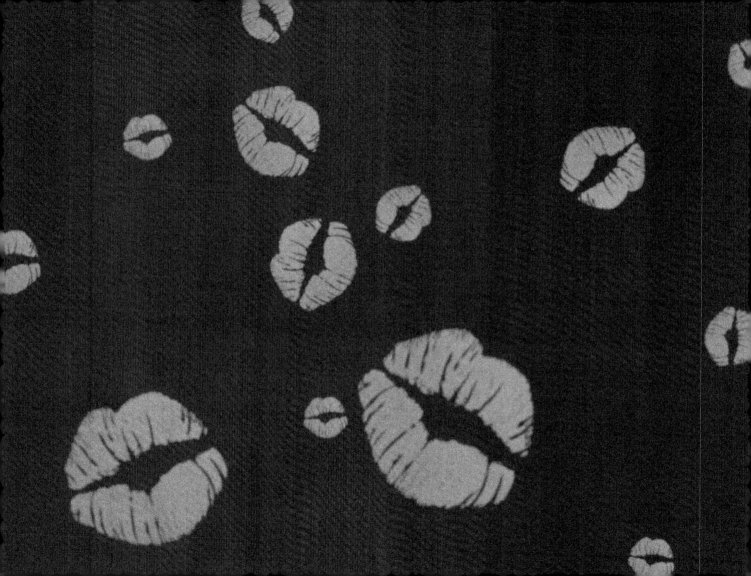

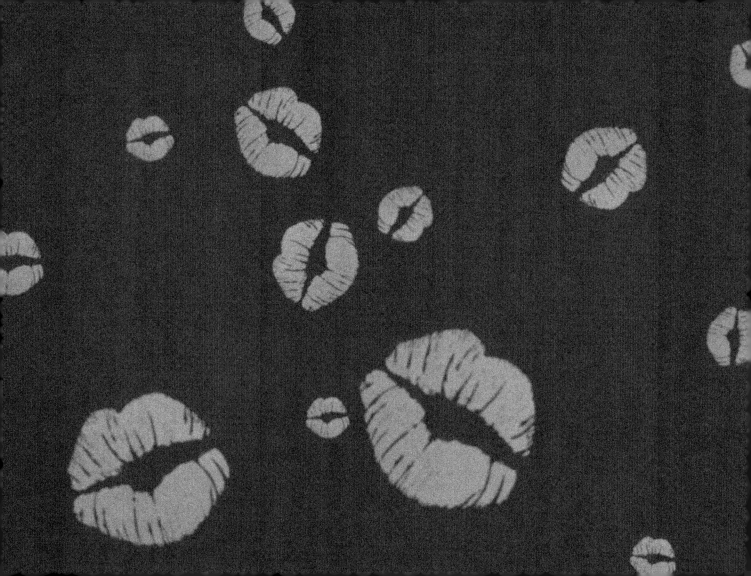

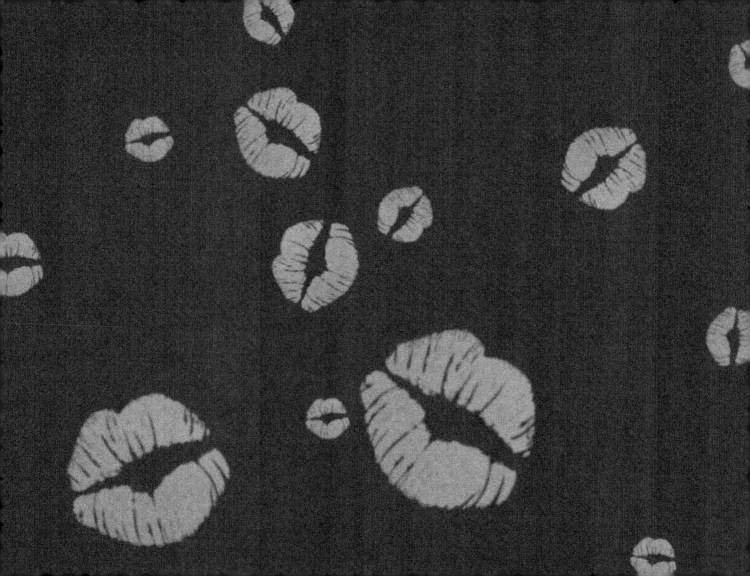

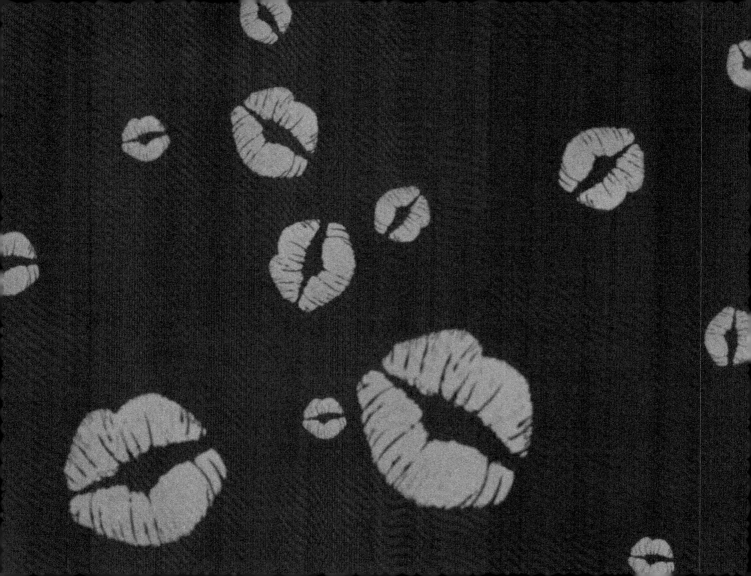

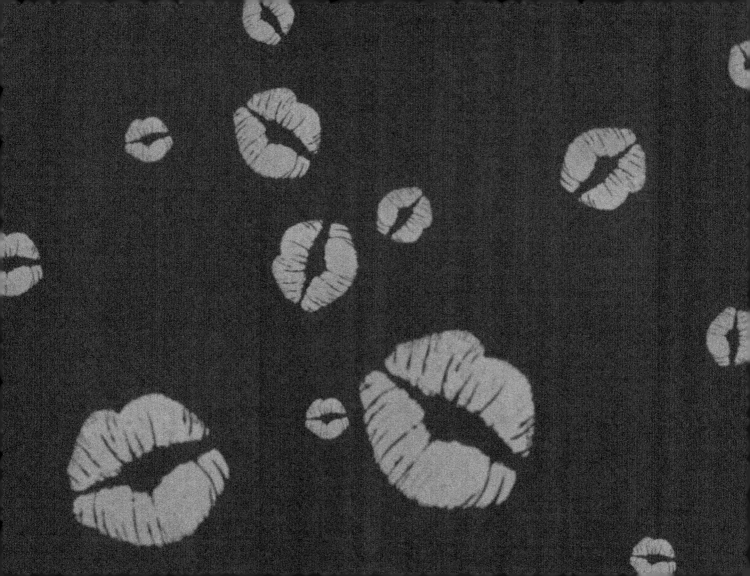

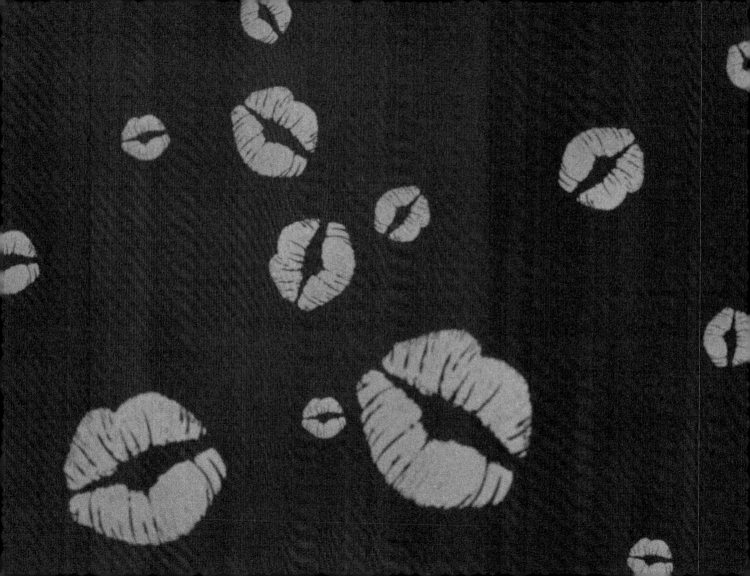

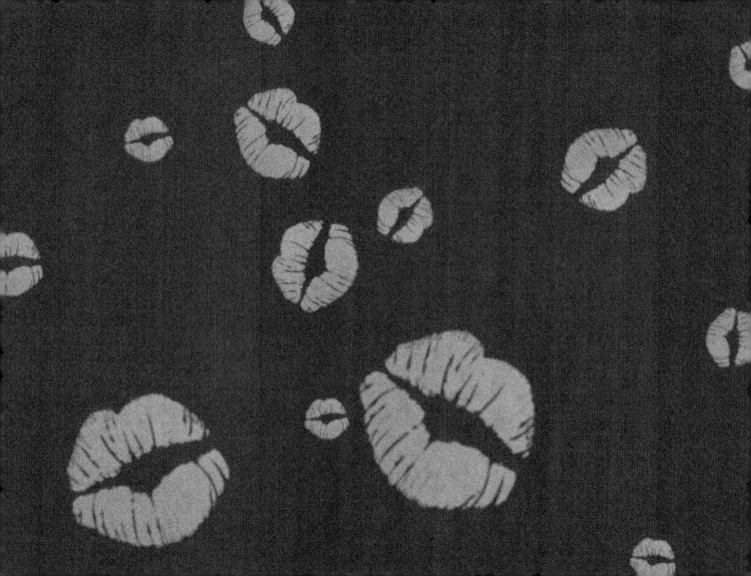

Printed in Great Britain
by Amazon

33388384R00071